BEFORE
THE SCHOOL BELL
RINGS

Also by Marjory Goldfinch Ward

Who Will Be *My* Teacher? Affirming Devotions
    for Teachers

BEFORE THE SCHOOL BELL RINGS

Devotions for Teachers

Marjory Goldfinch Ward

Baker Books

A Division of Baker Book House Co
Grand Rapids, Michigan 49516

Published by Baker Books
a division of Baker Book House Company
P.O. Box 6287, Grand Rapids, MI 49516-6287

Printed in the United States of America

Library of Congress Cataloging-in-Publication Data

Ward, Marjory G. (Marjory Goldfinch)
  Before the school bell rings : devotions for teachers / Marjory Goldfinch Ward.
     p.   cm.
  ISBN 0-8010-1127-2 (cloth)
  1. Teachers—Prayer-books and devotions—English.
2. Education (Christian theology)—Meditations. 3. Devotional calendars. I. Title
BV4596.T43W36   1996
242'.68—dc20   96-3219

For my beloved husband,
who is my teacher
too

THE LORD IS MY TEACHER

Paraphrase of the Twenty-Third Psalm

The Lord is my teacher,
I shall lack nothing.
He makes me sit down in
a comfortable place.
He leads me to relax and listen.
He quickens my mind.
He guides me along paths
of careful instruction
for the sake of his reputation
as a teacher.
Even though I walk
through difficult testing,
I will fear no failure,
for you, my teacher, are with me.
Your discipline and your encouragement
comfort me.

You prepare a place of acceptance for me
in the presence of my detractors.
You point me out with pride;
my cup of validation overflows.
Surely your goodness and kindness
will follow me,
all the days of my life,
and I will know myself also a teacher,
who follows your pattern of excellence
forever.

CONTENTS

PREFACE

In an interview after the publication of my book *Who Will Be My Teacher?* a reporter asked me, "How can a teacher be a Christian in a public school?"

I have seen so many Christian teachers in public schools that I was surprised at the question. Somehow we have gotten the impression that the separation of church and state means the total absence of any kind of religious presence in the public arena. Nothing could be further from the truth.

The young reporter and I discussed the distinction between living out the reality of who you are and proselytizing, or seeking to win people to a particular religious persuasion. Everyone who goes into a classroom—students, teachers, administrators, parents, visitors—brings with him or her the beliefs, values, character, and life experiences that uniquely belong to that individual. I have seen in public schools many teachers whose lives are filled with love, joy, peace, patience, kindness, goodness, faithfulness, gentleness, and self-control. Against such characteristics there can be no law (Gal. 5:22).

A first-grade teacher said wistfully, "I long for the day when I can read a Bible story to my students and know that I don't have to keep looking over my shoulder in case someone disapproves." Perhaps one day in our country, as in the Russian Commonwealth of 1992, Bible stories can be read as part of the literary heritage of our culture. But for now this loving teacher brings the truth of God's love into her classroom in the way she relates to the children. I wrote this book to help you do the same.

INTRODUCTION

Before my retirement, I taught in the education department of a women's college where many of the students are preparing to become teachers. A formidable array of skills is required for teaching. Preparation has to be intense. Working alongside an experienced teacher plays a significant role in the training of future teachers. Student teachers watch, listen, assist, and for short intervals take over the classroom.

A crucial element in this process is the selection of the "master teachers" who will train these students effectively. Part of this training is role modeling: "Watch what I do, and adapt it to your own teaching style."

If the relationship between the master teacher and the trainee is positive, the developing teacher leaves with a mixture of regret and excitement—regret at leaving a successful working relationship and excitement at the prospect of being on his or her own.

Many times the experienced teacher will urge, "Call me if you need me." In some places,

13

a computer networking system is available so that a new teacher can contact someone in a similar situation for advice with a particular problem.

As Christians who teach, we have master teacher resources available to us, even without computers!

Jesus is the master teacher who said, "Anyone who has faith in me will do what I have been doing" (John 14:12). The Holy Spirit is the one who comes alongside to guide us into truth and to make active in our lives the characteristics of Christ's own life (John 14:26; Gal. 5:22–23). And in Psalm 32:8 God the Father is described as our teacher: "I will instruct you and teach you in the way you should go; I will counsel you and watch over you."

When this great teaching team leads us into the classroom, we become teachers who reflect the love and power of God.

Each devotional in this book may be read in a quiet moment on Sunday or early Monday morning "before the school bell rings," serving as a seed planted for later bloom in that week's interaction with students.

May God bless you as you go out each day to make a difference in the life of someone in your classroom.

You are the light of the world. A city on a hill
cannot be hidden. . . . Let your light shine
before [children] that they may see your good
deeds and praise your Father in heaven.

Matthew 5:14, 16

Father, Son, and Holy Spirit,
   Thank you for teaching me.
   Grant that my teaching
may reflect your presence in my life.

1

"LIFT ME UP!"

He lifted them up and carried them all the days
of old.

Isaiah 63:9

In a vast crowd in Havana, a group of vis-
iting preachers from the United States watched
a parade going down a crowded street. As
tourists, they had been warned repeatedly to
be on guard against pickpockets and beggars,
many of whom were children.

Feeling a tug on his coattails, one preacher
looked down at a small boy wearing a huge
sombrero. His brown eyes pleaded as he
repeatedly asked something in Spanish, end-
ing with "Por favor, señor."

Reluctant to be victimized by a thief, the
American brushed the child away. The child's
plea did not register until later that evening
when the preacher realized to his horror that

the child had been begging, "Please sir, lift me up so I can see!"

All of us know how difficult it can be to have children crowding around, pulling at us, asking endless questions, making ceaseless demands with no consideration of all the other things we have to do. We hope the children will understand when we brush them off. We try to explain away the apparent rejection.

In our teaching, sometimes we forget to take the time to really listen to what a child is asking. Sometimes we don't listen to what a child is saying because we have already made up our mind about the child, as had the American pastor in Havana.

Sometimes we don't see a child because we are looking only at ourselves. We have needs too, and we often feel like children whose needs have not been met.

Jesus himself was once a child. With the help of his parents and other teachers, he "increased in wisdom (in broad and full understanding), and in stature and years, and in favor with God and man" (Luke 2:52 AMP).

What if you had been one of Jesus' teachers? You are, every day, for he said:

> Whoever welcomes a little child like this in my name welcomes me.
>
> Matthew 18:5

Whatever you did for one of the least of these
brothers of mine, you did for me.

Matthew 25:40

Stop and listen to your students. Put aside
the opinions you have formed in order to hear
what they are really saying. You may be pleas-
antly surprised at what you hear.

Our Father,
How did the rabbis
in the synagogue school
see your son, Jesus,
with his sparkling brown eyes
and eager questions?
How would they have taught him,
if they had known who he was?
Forgive me that too often
I have not seen him in the children
who don't look like him at all.
Help me to welcome the children
who come to me
and to listen to them with new ears.

2

"PLEASE LEARN MY NAME"

And the LORD said to Moses . . . I am pleased
with you and I know you by name.

Exodus 33:17

Those who know your name will trust in you,
for you, LORD, have never forsaken those
who seek you.

Psalm 9:10

A young child, just learning the Lord's Prayer,
said, "Our Father who art in heaven, how do
you know my name?"

I try to learn my students' names as quickly
as possible. Index cards in order of seating help
me to keep the names straight. Each semester
brings a changeover of eighty students. I'm
always glad when a student from a former class
comes in because I already know her name.

I learn names more quickly when I have encounters outside of class with students, when I have shared a problem, a joke, or a mutual acquaintance with them, when there's a personal connection.

Some of my students have shared their pain with me. When they invite me into their suffering, I do not easily forget their names.

Last summer a tornado struck a town near us. Teachers in a day care center heard the warning, woke up the napping children, led them to a central room, and made a game of getting under the tables. The teachers protected the children with their own bodies. They led the children in singing songs until rescuers arrived. All of them were safe because of the calm courage of the teachers.

The children knew their teachers. They listened when the teachers woke them up, called their names, and took them to safety. The trust relationship had been established. This trust protected the children.

Jesus said, "I am the good shepherd. The good shepherd lays down his life for the sheep. . . . I know my sheep and my sheep know me" (John 10:11, 14). Jesus knows my name. He knows the name of every one of my students. How does he know our names? He enters with us into the good times, the bad times, the dangers, the pain,

and the loss. And because Jesus is the Good
Shepherd, we know that when we hear his
voice, we can trust where he leads us.

> The name of the LORD is a strong tower;
> the righteous run to it and are safe.
>   Proverbs 18:10

> He calls his own sheep by name and leads them
> out. . . . His sheep follow him because they
> know his voice.
>
>   John 10:3–4

Father to the fatherless,
  Thank you that my mother told me
                your name.
You have always been my loving Father.
  You have never abandoned me
         and you never will.
Jesus said that he would not
     leave us comfortless,
      as orphans in a storm.
Show us who know you as Father
how to comfort and reassure the children
   who feel orphaned and abandoned
    in the terror of their uncertainties.
  May we help them to understand
 that you do, indeed, know the name
        of each one of us.

3

PLANT ACORNS

So, I believe in acorns; this is a part of my
teacher's creed.

                              Gerhard Frost

Other seed fell on good soil, where it pro-
duced a crop.

                              Matthew 13:8

Katherine came to her assigned school eager
to begin her student teaching but a little anx-
ious about what she might encounter. For
most of her life, since her own first-grade experience, she had planned to become a teacher.

When Katherine met Mrs. Martin, whom
she would assist, Mrs. Martin asked her,
"Why did you want to become a first-grade
teacher?"

Katherine answered, "Because of *my* first-grade teacher!"

Mrs. Martin inquired, "Where did you go to school, and who was that first-grade teacher?"

When Katherine told her, Mrs. Martin laughed delightedly. "That was my great-aunt!"

That veteran teacher who taught Katherine twenty-one years earlier could not have known that the "acorn" of love she planted in one child's life would become an "oak tree" for other children. Planting acorns was simply her way of life as a teacher.

Ann and Amy were shy, quiet twin girls whose mother had to go to prison when the girls were only four years old. They came timidly into their kindergarten classes, separated for the first time in their young lives. Their teachers welcomed them warmly; quickly the girls felt at home and began to learn eagerly. Both teachers planted acorns of love.

A friend of mine struggles with the meaning of the word *love*. He prefers to use the word *value* when speaking of love. My mother, as a public school teacher and as a Bible teacher, lived out that concept. Her students knew that she valued them.

Many years after my mother died, I visited one of her former students, who is now a distinguished professor of English at a state university. He picked up a battered, inexpensive Bible from his desk and showed me the inscription in my mother's handwriting. She had given a Bible to him and to each of the boys she had taught in an afternoon Bible club.

More than fifty years after receiving the Bible, this professor told me that he had drifted away from God after he had left home. "But for seven years I could not get away from your mother's belief that God exists. I returned to him, and in every class I have ever taught, I have used this Bible."

When my mother died, many people came to say, "She loved me." She planted acorns, and they bore fruit.

The tiny acorns of love and patience planted by teachers can grow into mighty oaks in the lives of their students, producing confident, caring individuals who in turn produce loving relationships of their own.

But the one who received the seed that fell on good soil is the man who hears the word and understands it. He produces a crop, yielding a hundred, sixty or thirty times what was sown.

Matthew 13:23

Father,
        The oak tree is not aware
        of the acorns falling from it.
    Many oak trees, countless acorns.
    Not all of the acorns fall into soft,
                ready places,
            but some of them do—
        enough to make a difference,
            enough to guarantee
that there will be oak trees in our future.
        I too cannot be conscious
        of where the acorns fall.
I must trust you with what I do in my life,
        the place where I am planted,
        and the crop that is produced.

4

WATCH ME WALK!

The boundary lines have fallen for me in
pleasant places;
surely I have a delightful inheritance.
Psalm 16:6

A Chinese woman saved every pair of
shoes that brought her through hard places,
and she described her life's journey as "walking in lucky shoes." She chose to be thankful for and to remember the difficulties
through which she had come.

I have students who wear "lucky shoes"
given to them by loving parents in a secure
environment. They walk steadily, joyfully,
and even dance on the path! They have been
given a "delightful inheritance."

Other students make their own shoes lucky
by letting their shoes carry them through
tough places, walking without fainting,
persevering, and giving thanks rather than
complaining.

Anita Shepard was born with Golden-Har syndrome, a birth defect that disfigured her face and twisted her body. With the support of cheerful and devoted parents, she has gone through repeated surgeries and difficult adjustments. She tackles her life with great energy and joy. When she sings solos in church, she gives praise to God, saying, "I give thanks—for someone to thank!"

When I try on my shoes to walk through my life and its circumstances, I choose to complain or to give thanks. Paul said, "I have learned to be content whatever the circumstances" (Phil. 4:11). He wrote those words from jail, and his letter is an epistle of joy. Giving thanks is a choice.

We love it when our students tell us we make a difference! But how many times do I thank a student for even the small things that make a difference in my classroom? At times we'd like to restore the privilege of spanking to the classroom. Perhaps a rash of thanking would work better. We may need a new bumper sticker: "Have you thanked a student today?"

You can make your shoes "lucky" by being thankful. A spirit of thankfulness will help us, and help us help others, through tough spots.

Father,
Thank you for my lucky shoes,
for love that met me at every turn,
work to do, and strength to get it done.
When the going gets rough,
Help me to keep on walking.
Help me to trudge faithfully
over rough places
and even to sing as the pilgrims sang
on their way to the Celestial City.
Give me a spirit of thankfulness
not just to you
for your vast mercies
and small continuing kindnesses
and constant giving,
but also to those tiny hands
or hulking awkward bodies
that timidly or clumsily bring
to me small mercies:
a courtesy
an effort
a generous act.
May I be more acute
to see the gesture I can thank
than I am to see the error I can rebuke
and so encourage my students
on their way.

5

CELEBRATE DIFFERENCES

The sun has one kind of splendor, the moon another and the stars another; and star differs from star in splendor.

1 Corinthians 15:41

In South Carolina, where I live, standard full meal fare offers rice and sweet potatoes. When I went to college in Illinois I ate boiled potatoes. When I lived in Virginia I found sweet potatoes but no rice.

At Thanksgiving, is it stuffing or dressing? made with cornbread and sage or white bread and oregano? Every cook has his or her own opinion.

What meals would your students plan for Thanksgiving?

Turkey? ham? both?
Oriental rice?

Mexican beans and tortillas?
Vegetarian alternatives?
Thin soup and poverty?

However the meal is constituted, from the simplest fare to the most bewildering array of choices, with thankful hearts we feast. However our students vary, we thank God for each one and for their differences.

A poster on a colleague's door portrays children of many nationalities with the caption: Everyone smiles in the same language.

As believers . . . don't show favoritism. Has not God chosen those who are poor in the eyes of the world to be rich in faith and to inherit the kingdom he promised those who love him?
James 2:1, 5

Father,
> *Our differences are obvious;*
> *we can scarcely ignore them.*
> *We naturally prefer others*
> *to be like ourselves,*
> *to make us comfortable and at ease*
> *with each other.*
> *We tend to value appearances*
> *and make judgments poorly.*

Grant us wisdom to know how
to celebrate our differences
in order to accept each other
and to fit into the beautiful mosaic
of your design.
May we remember as we gather
at your table
that you call us
from every tribe and nation
to bring praise and honor to you.

6

HELP ME
TO GIVE MYSELF

This is how we know what love is: Jesus Christ laid down his life for us. And we ought to lay down our lives for our brothers.

I John 3:16

And live a life of love, just as Christ loved us and gave himself up for us as a fragrant offering and sacrifice to God.

Ephesians 5:2

Thou that has given so much to me, give one thing more, a grateful heart. . . . Not thankful, when it pleaseth me, As if thy blessings had spare dayes: But such a heart, whose pulse may be Thy praise.

George Herbert
"Gratefulness"

Jenny, the five-year-old daughter of Rich Biega, a campus minister, once asked her father, "Why do we have turkey on Thanksgiving?"

Her father quickly launched into a homily on the early settlers, their hard first year, and their thankful hearts when they sat down together to share their harvest. After describing this first Thanksgiving, he added that sometime later someone had the splendid idea of adding the turkey as the centerpiece for the feast.

Jenny looked up at her father. "I'm not sure what you mean."

Patiently, her father explained again about the feast and the welcome addition of the turkey. Jenny interrupted him impatiently, "That's not very nice for the bird!"

The centerpiece of the feast was an unwilling sacrifice for the good of the family. "Thanks" is part of the special day. "Giving" is the other part. The turkey gives everything; the family gives thanks!

Ideally, I am a willing sacrifice for the good of my students, as I place my life—my energy, my attention, my love—on the "table" before my students. Some days, however, I may feel more like the turkey, whose sacrifice is demanded but not welcomed.

Do my students give thanks in my classroom? Do I have to become the "sacrificial centerpiece" for this to happen?

One of my students came to me today with tears in her eyes, saying, "I need a hug."

Her son's former girlfriend was in the hospital expecting his child. Her cousin's eighteen-year-old daughter recently died of ovarian cancer. And the doctor had just told my student that she might have leukemia. She plans to student teach and graduate next semester. I need to give her a lot of hugs.

Officer Cruz and his partner are assigned to a police station in the center of a low-income apartment complex. Their presence has helped to change that neighborhood from one of constant violence and drug dealing to one where the children run out to meet the squad car, calling to the policeman, grabbing his leg, clinging to him. When Officer Cruz visits their school, they gather around him, delighted to see him.

The police officers open their station in the afternoon and provide volunteers to read to the children, to help them with their homework, and to give them cookies and Kool-Aid. The officers and volunteers choose to become willing sacrifices so that the children can feel safe and loved.

Greater love has no one than this, that he lay
down his life for his friends.

John 15:13

Father,

> *To give up my time,*
> *my energy,*
> *my attention,*
> *my love,*
> *my life itself without a thought*
> *of what it costs me—*
> *surely this is a sacrifice worthy to be called*
> *an act of praise that honors you*
> *who gave the ultimate sacrifice.*
> *I see the sacrifice as noble*
> *when I stand at a distance*
> *and think about it.*
> *When I am tired and feeling cranky*
> *I lose sight of the value*
> *and think only of the cost.*
> *Help me to follow Christ's example.*
> *Help me to think of others first,*
> *especially my students.*

7

SEIZE THE DAY!

Teach us to number our days aright,
that we may gain a heart of wisdom.
Psalm 90:12

"Once upon a time, and in a time we are now living, a little boy, deep in the deepest woods, found a very solemn and very small Indian." So begins Margaret Wise Brown's story, *David's Little Indian,* about an Indian who came to live with a boy named David. Together they found something special about every day. One day was "the day of the first nut that fell"; another, "the day it didn't snow."

The tiny Indian's name, he told David, was Carpe Diem, and David called him Carpe for short. "It was a wonderful life, that life of the boy and his Indian. And they grew up and never missed a day."

We slowed down when our grandchildren came so that we would "never miss a day." One day I watched a bug crawl across the sidewalk and lifted him carefully on a leaf to examine him more closely. My granddaughter Libby and I did not forget our "day the bug crawled on the leaf."

I remember one day in my first teaching experience (in a country schoolhouse with thirty-five second- and third-grade students) as "the day the ghosts came to school." My mother and my husband dressed in sheets and visited the classroom. One child jumped out of the window and ran home! (I can't recall what the objective of the lesson was for that day, but we accomplished something memorable.)

One day, when our children were young, we woke up to a cold house with no electricity or heat. My husband made a fire in the fireplace, and we centered our activities there for the day. That night during family prayers, small David did not mention the inconveniences. He said, "Thank you for the good fire." That was our "day of the good fire."

Every classroom and every home needs a "little Indian." What is your day today? Name it with the students!

I still find
each day too short
for all the thoughts
I want to think,
all the walks
I want to take,
all the books I want to read,
and all the friends
I want to see.

John Burroughs
greeting card

Father,
I have run past so many days,
not noticing the first nut that fell,
the first crocus that bloomed,
the first smile of a new baby.
I have run past so many "little Indians"
who would have come with me
to show me the specialness of each day.
Thank you that Jesus noticed everything—
the lilies of the field,
the sparrows flying and falling,
the two mites of a widow's offering.
Grant me sharp eyes like the little Indian
so that I may not miss the special gift
of each day.

8

GiVE THANKS WiTH A GRATEFUL HEART

Give thanks to the LORD, for he is good;
his love endures forever.

Psalm 107:1

Before the Thanksgiving holiday, a third-grade class made a large display of student posters illustrating all the things they were thankful for:

> I am really thankful for doctors, for they can help you from a very serious disease or being killed.
> For food—some kinds are very good—especially cantaloupe.
> For my hamster and parakeet, and clothes to wear at night and morning.
> Shelter or a home, to keep me safe when a bad storm comes.

40

For children—children are very special people.

For my life—and for football.

For schools to learn in—but not this one. I like my old school better.

For Mom and Dad, a cat, and a lunchbox.

For my treehouse and my daddy.

For my parents, my uncles, grandpas, and God.

I'm thankful for pigs so we can have meat.

For my dog named Ruffy.

For adults, the people I love—and sometimes my sister.

My friend Delores went through an agonizing three years caring for her teenage daughter Melanie before Melanie died at seventeen of brain stem cancer. During those years, and in the following years of grief, Dee has demonstrated the remarkable gift of gratitude. When her sorrow weighs her down, even the sight of a butterfly alighting delicately on a flower will lift her heart into praise. I have seen in her what the power of praise for even the smallest things can accomplish.

After supper at our house one night, our grandson Andrew went to his grandfather and hugged him. "Thank you, Granddaddy, for the very good soup."

A ten-year-old child knew the grace of gratitude for small things. We could all learn the same.

Every desirable and beneficial gift comes out of heaven. The gifts are rivers of light cascading down from the Father of Light.

James 1:17 *The Message*

Praise be to the LORD, the God of Israel,
from everlasting to everlasting.
Let all the people say, "Amen!"

Psalm 106:48

Father of Light, giver of all good things,
Thank you.

9

SHOW GOD'S KINGDOM

The kingdom of God is within you.
Luke 17:21

My grandchildren like to help me make
rolls. They stir the ingredients in a heavy pot
and then wait impatiently for the dough to
rise so that we can punch and roll and cut
and dip the circles into melted butter and
place them carefully in a pan. For two hours
we have to wait before the rolls have risen
enough to bake.

Sometimes I worry when the rolls don't
rise fast enough. I'm afraid the yeast was too
old, the water too hot, or I forgot some vital
ingredient. Once I left out the yeast until it
was almost too late to add it to the mixture.
If I hadn't caught my mistake in time, the
whole batch would have been ruined.

When I read the newspapers, I wonder if
the "yeast" of God's kingdom has been left

out of our world. A sodden lump of wickedness offers no hope of a righteous outcome.

People around Jesus shared this kind of discouragement. They wanted to know where they could look for God's kingdom. He answered, "The kingdom of God doesn't come by counting the days on the calendar. Nor when someone says, 'Look here!' or, 'There it is!' And why? Because God's kingdom is already among you" (Luke 17:20–21 *The Message*), or as the NIV states, "the kingdom of God is within you" (Luke 17:21).

God's kingdom is already within us and among us. Anywhere God is at work, using the hands of his people, God is there and the yeast of his kingdom is rising.

Just as making bread requires the busy hands of the baker, making God's kingdom evident in the world requires the hands of those who believe in him.

Some rise up and demand justice for the helpless. One of my students shared a story about her developmentally disabled sister. When her sister's special class presented a program at the school, her sister sat in her wheelchair and said, "Thank you for Public Law 94-142." Because of this law there have been major changes in the treatment of disabled individuals. People no longer overlook their needs in planning school programs, buildings, and services.

In our community, John Fling, known nationally for his work, feeds the hungry and clothes the poor.

On Thanksgiving Day, hundreds of volunteers serve meals to those who cannot provide meals for themselves.

In schools, armies of educators quietly do their work, making a difference in the lives of students.

A bad dream woke up four-year-old Colin in the middle of the night, and he crawled into bed with his mother. She tried to soothe him back to sleep. He asked, "Is Jesus bigger than all the monsters in the whole world? Does he smash the houses and beat the monsters with the sticks?"

"Well, no, not exactly," his mother answered. "But he finds a lot of other ways to take care of us."

After he saw *The Lion King,* Colin decided that God has an evil brother that makes all the monsters, but Jesus and God are bigger than the evil brother.

We are a lot older than Colin, but we'd like to see God take sticks and smash a few monsters. We are impatient with slowly rising yeast, and we want God to do something fast to solve the problems we have created.

What is the kingdom of God?
Where is the place where God rules?
How can I show my students such a
    place?
  With my hands,
  with my voice,
  in my classroom,
  in my life.

The news of God's kingdom is good news!

By this all men will know that you are my disciples, if you love one another.

John 13:35

Do not be afraid, little flock, for your Father has been pleased to give you the kingdom.

Luke 12:32

Father,
Thank you for the signs of your kingdom
  I see every day, in every place,
  when I know what to look for.
Thank you for your presence, your rule,
  in your quietly obedient servants.
    Thine is the kingdom,
    and the power,
    and the glory
    forever.

10

HELP ME FIND THE GIFT

As each has received a gift, employ it for one another.

1 Peter 4:10 RSV

Gifts pile up under the twinkling lights of the Christmas tree: small packages—big packages—inconspicuous packages—commanding packages—brown paper—striped paper—perfect wrappings—crude wrappings—childish scrawl—perfect script—fancy bows—string and ribbon—bright colors—torn wrappings—tempting piles of treasures.

After the gifts are opened with much excitement, the wrappings, tossed heedlessly aside in our haste to get to the real gift concealed inside, become trash to recycle or discard.

So it is with the gifts within children. Some children are packaged nicely: always neatly groomed, hair combed just so, curls tied back with a perky bow that stays in place all day. Others are thrown together: shoes grabbed in a hurry, shirts untucked, socks that don't match, hair uncombed. Inside each package is a unique gift for teacher to find.

Jamie sits beside the teacher's desk in his third-grade classroom. His teacher likes to keep her eye on him.

On my third or fourth visit, as I sat in the classroom observing the student teacher, Jamie sidled up beside me and gave me a big hug. Now whenever I visit, Jamie grins and comes over for a hug.

I have no idea how well he does in class. From what I have seen, he isn't too deeply involved in academics. But I do know that Jamie has a "people gift" to be treasured.

Miss Estelle had such a gift. Once when I visited her, she said wistfully, "All I know how to do is to love people!" Miss Estelle never married; her family consisted of her aging parents whom she nursed to the end of their lives, her sister, and her nieces and nephews, whose care she shared and who adored her. Wherever she went, she spilled love and encouragement on every person she saw, regardless of how he or she looked on the outside. She never considered her love a particular gift, just a spontaneous impulse.

Some students have academic gifts that fit well in any classroom. Others, like Jamie, have people gifts that fit well anywhere. I have to believe that every student *is* a gift, and *has* a gift that will fit in my classroom and my life. But sometimes I need help in overlooking the packaging!

Go after a life of love as if your life depended on it—because it does. Give yourselves to the gifts God gives you. Trust steadily in God, hope unswervingly, love extravagantly. And the best of the three is love.

1 Corinthians 14:1; 13:13 *The Message*

Father,
Thank you for Miss Estelle.
Thank you that she shared her gift of love
and saw it grow and grow and bless every
life she touched.
Thank you for Jamie.
Thank you for his cheerful smile
and his ready hugs.
Thank you for the gift stored up
in every child.
Help me to look beyond the "wrappings"
to find the gift inside each one.

11

TAKE ME
TO THE MANGER

Today in the town of David a Savior has been
born to you; he is Christ the Lord. This will
be a sign to you: You will find a baby wrapped
in cloths and lying in a manger.

Luke 2:11–12

Our grandson Andrew played the part of
Joseph in the kindergarten Christmas pag-
eant. He took his responsibility very seriously;
he would not even glance in our direction.
He knew that Joseph was a main character,
but he told us solemnly that the child who
had the biggest part of all was the one who
shook the star that pointed the way to Jesus.
Each child in that scene felt the significance
of each role.

As the children stand around the manger, I think about the roles they are playing. Mary was young when the angel visited her. She accepted the mystery and thought about it for the rest of her life as she fed and clothed and nurtured her son.

Joseph did what he was told to do. He stuck it out, day by day, raising this miracle child, being husband to this wife who had been greatly honored by God. Joseph was a working man, faithful to the task God gave him. He never made the headlines, but he was chosen for a vital part: the role model of "father" for the Son of God.

The shepherds were also working men, not expecting anything unusual that night. When the message came, they dropped everything and rushed to see the one who had been announced. What happened to them after that? Were their lives forever different?

The innkeeper also had his working hours interrupted. So far as we know, he took no notice of the strange happenings near his establishment.

Herod actively tried to destroy the child. He refused to allow the threat of any competition for his throne.

The wise men saw the star and followed its light to the king they sought. It took a long time. They did not arrive at the manger but found the house where Mary and Joseph and Jesus went to live. They persisted in their journey and brought unusual, valuable gifts that indicated their reverence for royalty.

Where will the children standing around this manger take their stand in life?

Like the innkeeper, will they never realize the miracle's significance in their lives while it happens all around them?

Like Mary and Joseph, will they enter into the mystery and provide a home for Jesus?

Like Herod, will they turn against him and insist on running their own lives?

Like the shepherds, will they welcome the news and rush off to confirm the message for themselves?

Like the wise men, will they search for him a long time and bring him their unique gifts?

How about me? Can I come to the manger, pondering the mystery, and bring the children with me?

> The shepherds returned, glorifying and praising God for all the things they had heard and seen, which were just as they had been told.
>
> Luke 2:20

Father,
We are losing the impact
of the Christmas story
in our schools and in our lives.
If we cannot introduce the children
to the Christ child,
how will they learn who he is?
As I come to the manger
to worship the Christ child,
show me how to bring the children
so that they can hear the angels sing.

12

DO SMALL THINGS

My command is this: Love each other as I
have loved you.

John 15:12

One of my college students came to me
after class one day, smiling bravely as she held
back tears. Hesitantly, she said, "I was . . .
assaulted last week." In the intervening days
she had missed her classes, trying to get her
life back together after a betrayal by one she
thought she could trust.

There was no "big thing" I could do: erase
the memory, make it not have happened,
restore her body to innocence. All I could
offer were words and gestures, small attempts
to treat deep wounds.

There are big issues stalking our culture.
Racial and personal tensions erupt in violence in our schools and public places, as well
as in the home environment. Children are

scarred by events they are not prepared to understand.

I don't know how to ease these tensions; prevent violence; combat hatred, resentment, and insensitivity. But I can love one child and make a difference, at least to that child.

A student named Sandra wrote to her teacher, "You make God's love real." The teachers that I remember did no big things for me. They could not. But they came to school every day; they taught me what I needed to learn. And when I needed understanding and encouragement, they gave it to me. In their attitude they made God's love real.

One of my colleagues cried in frustration,

How can I teach young women when their lives are in turmoil, when they don't know where they belong or who will be at home tonight, or will they even have a home tomorrow, when they're dealing with rampant sex pressures, inner conflicts, and the threat of violence and death? I see in a student's eyes the desperate question, "What does it matter how I pronounce a word, or what it means, when I don't even know what my life means, or if it means anything at all?"

The twelve whom Jesus taught faced insurmountable problems. He prepared them, little by little, precept by precept, and told them,

"You don't understand it now, but you will understand it later."

Little by little. Small tasks, steady faithfulness, building character by instruction and example. Can I believe that this will, in fact, make a difference?

Mother Teresa said, "We can do no great things—only small things with great love."

Father,
You know how many great things need
to be done.
You see the frustration of our helplessness.
Thank you for the small things we can do.
Thank you for every encounter in each day.
You know how easy it is to overlook
small kindnesses
and worry overmuch about large threats.
Our world is tuned to BIG—numbers,
people, events.
We blow up the insignificant
and make it sensational.
You make small things significant.
You will not overlook even tiny sparrows
sold two for a penny.
Show me how to see sparrows and care,
without grief that hurts
more than I can bear.

13

SET THE RIGHT STANDARD

The law of the LORD is perfect,
reviving the soul.
The statutes of the LORD are trustworthy,
making wise the simple.

Psalm 19:7

I signed the visitors' register at an elementary school and noticed that several people had signed in ahead of me using the wrong date. I checked the list and the calendar to make sure that I was not mistaken. The first ones in that day had marked correctly "January 26." Someone then came in and wrote beside her name "January 27." Those who followed automatically picked up her error.

As I left the school, I signed out, noting that those who followed me had followed my example, using the correct date again.

It was such a small matter, but it affected me. The day before I had talked with the assistant principal of another school. Deeply troubled for the children, she had said, "Our problems mount. Every day we see more distressed children. They have behavior problems, learning problems, emotional problems. Everybody expects the schools to solve all the problems. We can't do it. Each person has to become responsible for his own decisions."

Responsibility. Before I act or play copycat I have to learn how to stop and think, *Why am I doing this? Is it right? What is my standard for this action?*

When I sensed that the date was wrong, I had a calendar to check. I did not have to write the wrong date simply because a list of people before me wrote it that way.

Why is it that we can agree that this date is right and that one is wrong, and we can't tell the children that this action is right and that one is wrong? How are they supposed to find out?

What St. Augustine called a "divine sense of oughtness" lies in each human spirit. We simply know that some behaviors are right and other behaviors are wrong. We also know that we are accountable to someone beyond ourselves. To deny these realities is to confuse children in the deepest part of their inner selves.

Kindness is right.

Cruelty is wrong.
Love is right.
Hatred is wrong.
We do not have to be afraid to tell the students that some things are right and other things are wrong. They know it already, especially when they are victims of the wrong. We can encourage them to "check it out" before automatically following the example of someone else.

We also need to do our own checking out. When I walk into the teachers' lounge and hear complaining and criticizing, do I automatically add my voice to the chorus? or can I steer the conversation in another direction?

When I sit down to eat in the cafeteria or at home, do I notice immediately what's wrong with the food? After years of cooking meals for my family, I sympathize with those who have to cook for anybody else. No matter how carefully they plan and prepare, they rarely please everybody who eats.

When others lament the behaviors of "terrible students," can I point out the positive actions I have seen? Each of us in the schools knows that the bad behaviors are the work of a few individuals. Most of the students are cooperative, conscientious, and helpful. They should be congratulated at least as often as the difficult students are criticized.

When their grandfather picked up Libby and Andrew after school, Andrew said, "Libby, I saw your name on the list today. You were 'caught being good!' What did you do?" Their school actively looks for the good things students do. On his report card, Andrew's teacher had written, "Thank you for helping the Spanish student with his work."

How confusing for us all if each of us could choose the calendar date we preferred today. How difficult for us all if each of us could be a law unto himself or herself today.

Choose what is right! Your choice will encourage others to choose what is right too.

Do not merely listen to the word and so deceive yourselves. Do what it says.

James 1:22

Father,
  You have set the right standard for us.
    We ignore it to our own peril.
  When the children look at my life,
    may they see your standard in action.
      May I not have to be ashamed
         when they do what I do,
           say what I say,
and treat others the way I treat them.

14

TEACH ME
WHAT LOVE IS

No matter what I say, what I believe, and
what I do, I'm bankrupt without love.
1 Corinthians 13:2 *The Message*

When I was a child, I liked to twist the rope
of a swing and whirl around as it unwound.
I have since learned that to avoid dizziness
when whirling around you have to keep your
eyes fixed on an immovable object. I wish I
had known that when I was ten years old!

In our whirling world, what can I keep my
eyes fixed on? How can I keep from losing
my balance? How can I help my students
walk straight?

The only unchanging, unmovable factor in
our lives is God, who says of himself that he
is love. His love is unconditionally accepting,
as mine must be. But how does this love

express itself? Is it not one of Alice in Wonderland's "impossible things"?

Love is not a warm gush of affection that comes more easily for some students than for others. Love is behavior more than emotion. To check if you love people, ask yourself these questions:

Am I patient with them?
Am I kind to them?
Do I envy them?
Do I boast of my own accomplishments?
Am I proud, and do I consider myself better than they are?
Am I rude to them?
Do I seek what is best for me, or for them?
Do I get angry with them?
Do I keep a record of their wrongs against me?
Do I revel when others have to grovel?
Do I look for the best in others?
Do I trust?
Do I hope?
Do I persevere, or give up?
Am I childish?

"Making this list and checking it twice" we can get a good idea of where the weak places are in our love for other people.

He who loves his fellowman has fulfilled the law.

Romans 13:8

Father,
Thank you that you love
us completely,
eternally,
unconditionally.
Thank you that you are patient and kind
and never give up on any one
of your children.
Keep my attention centered
on you who are love,
so that in this whirling world
I may not lose my balance and fall down
into the dirt.

15

GIVE THEM HOPE

For I know the plans I have for you, declares the LORD, plans to prosper you and not to harm you, plans to give you hope and a future.

Jeremiah 29:11

He who began a good work in you will carry it on to completion until the day of Christ Jesus.

Philippians 1:6

In my senior year in high school, I was in Miss Alma Lewis's English class. Miss Alma knew English and she knew how to teach it. Once you met her standards, you could use the English language correctly.

I worked hard on my term paper that year. The day after Miss Alma corrected the paper, she asked me to stay after class. When the other students had left, Miss Alma handed me the paper and said in her dignified way, "I think you should consider a career in journalism."

Her comment planted an idea in my mind, a hope for my future, that I never forgot. Miss Alma was the first to see that I had the potential to become a writer.

Years later, when my former teacher approached her 100th birthday, I went to the nursing home to see her. She asked me to stand in a strong light so that even with her failing eyesight she could see me. Pleased, she said, "Now I can see my Marjory!" Forty years had passed and she could still find glimpses of her student in my face.

I had other teachers who gave me hope and made a time commitment in order to build on their confidence in me. They were nurturers as well as teachers.

What do I foresee for my students?

What do I point them toward?

What potential do I see in them?

Have you ever thought, *That student will never amount to anything*? Your thought made a difference in the way you taught that student and in the way the student learned.

Nathaniel Hawthorne wrote, "Life is made up of marble and mud." Some teachers see the marble; others see the mud.

There is surely a future hope for you,
and your hope will not be cut off.
Proverbs 23:18

Father,
Your prophet Samuel anointed
a shepherd boy
because you saw David as a king
after your own heart.
Your Son, Jesus, chose twelve men
no one else would have chosen
for leadership
because you saw that they would
turn the world upside down.
I don't have eyes to see what you see
in my students.
Show me the hidden riches within them,
or let me believe that potential is there
beyond anything I can imagine.
Let me believe in them
so that they can believe in themselves.
Let me give them hope
beyond what they have seen for themselves.

16

TEST ME

I know, my God, that you test the heart and
are pleased with integrity.

1 Chronicles 29:17

One part of the teaching process I don't like
is testing and grading. I want standards hard
enough to be challenging, that demand rigor-
ous attention and effective learning. But I want
standards to be realistic enough for all students to be successful. Part of me wants to be
tough and demanding. Part of me wants to be
accepting and understanding.

I look for new and better ways to teach and
test. If I can figure out exactly what is going
on in a student's mind, causing an error to be
made, then I can address that problem. Was
the question unclear? Did the student understand the information? Did the student study?

Students will vigorously defend their
answers if they are convinced that they are
right or that I was unfair.

What about my attitude toward God's expectations in my life? Can I defend myself to him? Suppose I am convinced that he is unfair? or that his standards are cold and unfeeling, impossible to meet? or that they do nothing but harm me?

One of our professors is known for his tough standards. He expects students to take good notes and study thoroughly. Some of them fail repeatedly. A former student came back recently to say thank you to him. She had been required to repeat his course in order to graduate, and she had been less than happy about that. But twenty years later she has a teenager of her own about whom she said to the professor, "I realized that I could understand what is happening to him because of what I learned in your course. I came back to thank you. I didn't enjoy the tough time I had in the class, but I knew you cared about what happened to me." She learned that tough standards can be a blessing in life.

God has good reasons for his tough standards, just as teachers do. Teachers set high standards to help students reach full and successful lives—lives with good jobs and knowledge about the world, just as God sets high standards to help us obtain full and successful lives—lives of peace and freedom.

God's standards, impossible as they seem, cannot be changed. To do so would alter God's plan for balanced, healthy, and successful living. The Ten Commandments were not ten suggestions.

What are God's expectations? We are to act justly, love mercy, and walk humbly with our God (Micah 6:8). Jesus told us to "love your enemies and pray for those who persecute you" (Matt. 5:44). How can we ever pass these tests?

Jesus as our teacher sets impossible standards for us, but Jesus as our redeemer changes us into the kind of people who can meet the objectives in his curriculum.

> Search me, O God, and know my heart;
> test me and know my anxious thoughts.
> See if there is any offensive way in me,
> and lead me in the way everlasting.
> Psalm 139:23–24

Father,
 I know that you sent us Jesus,
  the perfect teacher.
You gave to him the right curriculum.
You know that his standards are impossibly
  high for me.

But you also sent him to be our
perfect redeemer.
He came, not only to teach us,
but to make us good.
I need to have high expectations
for my students.
For their good, they need to measure up.
I wish that I could also change
in my students
everything that blocks their learning:
disabilities, lack of preparation,
inadequate motivation,
pressing distractions, difficult material—
the problems that bring down test scores.
I'm glad you grade differently.
You understand me, deeply and completely.
Give me an understanding heart
for my students.
Give me the grace to do everything
that I can
to make it possible for them to learn well.
Give me grace also to accept the fact
that I can't do everything,
and to trust you to make up the difference.

17

REST AWHILE

> Come to me, all you who are weary and burdened, and I will give you rest. Take my yoke upon you and learn from me, for I am gentle and humble in heart, and you will find rest for your souls. For my yoke is easy, and my burden is light.
>
> Matthew 11:28–30

The first time I went to the library at Chapin Elementary School I saw an old claw-foot bathtub piled with pillows, used as a center of quiet for children to curl up and read a favorite book in. When I saw it, I thought, *If there had been one of these in our old Conway Elementary School library, I'd still be there reading!*

I never actually saw a child in the old bathtub, in that school or in any of the other schools I visited, even though several of the libraries had a similar setup. I'm sure that the children used the special places, but I never saw one used.

When I see the frantic pace of our lives—harried teachers, distressed parents, restless children, burdened administrators, harassed legislators struggling with school issues, I want to say, "Find the quiet place and crawl into it!"

John and Charles Wesley's mother, with her thirteen children, managed to find time to spend alone with each child. She lacked modern conveniences, but she made full use of old-fashioned ones. She is quoted as saying that she made a quiet place for herself by throwing her apron over her head to pray.

Our aprons hang on the wall as quaint decorations. Most of our old clawfoot bathtubs have been replaced. We are plagued by attention deficit disorders in adults and in children. Some psychologists believe that at least some of the problem can be blamed on the fact that children are not expected to pay attention to adults. Few of us take time to listen, to God or to each other.

I may know that the "quiet place" is there for me, but it does me no good unless I crawl into it and listen.

> Be still, and know that I am God;
> I will be exalted among the nations,
> I will be exalted in the earth.
>
> Psalm 46:10

Father,
Getting still is hard for me.
I can blame all the clamor,
the demands,
the din and clatter of my life,
but I know that the real reasons
lie deeper than the surface clutter
of my life.
I remember Mary,
who came and sat down at Jesus' feet,
and Martha, who didn't.
Part of me wants to sit down and listen,
but the louder part of me wants
to get the job done.
My students can't sit in a bathtub
and read all the time.
They have to do their work.
Work is important.
Tune me in to that still, small voice,
your voice,
speaking so softly
that I have to get still enough to listen,
to hear you tell me
that work is not the same as keeping busy
and that resting in your quiet place
is essential to the real work
you have given me to do.

18

"DON'T PASS ME BY"

Let the little children come to me, and do not hinder them, for the kingdom of heaven belongs to such as these.

Matthew 19:14

James Limburg tells a story about a famous rabbi who was to be the featured speaker at a synagogue somewhere in Poland. As he came walking down the street, he heard a child crying, went into the house, picked up the crying baby, and sang a lullaby until the child fell asleep. The mother had left the crying baby and rushed to the synagogue to hear the rabbi.

When he arrived and the services could begin, the rabbi told the congregation about the crying baby, explaining, "After all, it is much easier for God to wait than for that child."

We too easily neglect the vulnerable child in order to tend to the system. This is not a modern phenomenon, unique to our hectic culture. When parents brought their children to Jesus for his blessing, the disciples would

74

have pushed them aside in their focus on urgent adult issues.

When I, irritable, burned out, sick of my job, face my class, one small distress is one too many. It can trigger such thoughts as these:

Get that child out of here!
Clean my room!
Don't give me another bus duty!
I must have a raise!
Listen to me!

These immediate issues can take us away from our concern for the children. Yet, our pain over them is real and may thinly cloak deep discouragement, even despair. Jesus hears the audible cry and reads the underlying scream of pain too.

Jesus always dealt kindly with the presenting problem. "Friends, haven't you any fish?" he asked (John 21:5).

Can I open the door and let in that hurting child even when my own responsibilities are mounting? Can I, like Jesus, listen for the silent pain as I deal with the immediate problem? This is asking a lot of me, when I have my own pressures to handle.

When I am close to him, I can remember, when I hear the cries of the children, that my own cries will not go unheard. Together we can be comforted by the God who puts first things first but understands our concern for what may be considered less important issues.

> Come to me, all you who are weary and burdened, and I will give you rest.
>
> Matthew 11:28

Father,
Too often I have wanted
to leave the crying child
and rush to the synagogue
where "important things" are taking place.
You know the pressing issues,
the "important things" I am
accountable for.
Forgive me when I neglect the child
in order to take care of the paperwork.
You understand why I get upset
over things that aren't very significant,
at least not to anybody else.
The kitchen mattered to Martha
more than it mattered to you and to Mary.
Thank you that you loved them both,
and understood their choices.
Thank you that you will help me deal
with my priorities too.

19

HONOR YOUR CONTRACT

I am the Lord's servant, Mary answered. May
it be to me as you have said.

Luke 1:38

As the eyes of a maid look to the hand of
her mistress,
so our eyes look to the LORD our God.

Psalm 123:2

Teachers are under contract. About most
duties there is little discussion. By signing the
contract I agree to comply with the expectations of the school board, the school district
administrators, and the principal of the
school where I work. If I don't like my contract I can break it or decide not to renew it,
but as long as I am under contract I have to
live up to the stated terms (even line thirteen,
". . . and any other duties assigned by the

supervisor"). I can comply and grumble, or I can comply and smile. But I must comply if I want to keep the job. I am a teacher under contract.

I also have a contract, or covenant, with God. He offers life everlasting and the sure promise of his faithfulness. I, in turn, out of gratefulness, live for him and serve him. I am God's servant. I can obey him and grumble, or I can obey him cheerfully, joyful that I have a master like God.

Once after I had visited another school district, I came back to my own superintendent and said fervently, "Thank you for my job! Thank you for letting me work here!" I look into the lined, sad faces of many people who "serve other masters," and I say fervently to God, "Thank you for letting me work for you! Thank you for the kind of master you are. Forgive me when I grumble about my assignments."

Gert Behanna, whose life God transformed after years of luxury, alcoholism, and brokenness, keenly felt her role as a grateful servant of God. Once, in a crowded bus station on her way to a speaking engagement, she went into a dirty public restroom, cleaned the stall and the mirror, and left, saying, "There, Lord, I hope you enjoy it!" She took seriously what he had said: "If you have done it for the least of these, you have done it for me" (Matt. 25:40 author's paraphrase).

The Bible describes our role as that of a maid to her mistress. The young maid was expected to keep her eyes on the hands of her mistress so that at the slightest gesture she could quickly jump to obey.

My son-in-law has trained his little dog to obey him. He speaks quietly and Terra obeys at once, even when she obviously does not want to obey.

We expect our students to obey quickly, to listen to the quiet, confident voice of authority. Can we do less ourselves? We are told that we are servants. What qualities make an excellent servant?

dependability
loyalty
obedience
a cheerful spirit
humility
gratitude

Our example is Jesus himself, who

made himself nothing,
    taking the very nature of a servant,

being made in human likeness.
And being found in appearance as a man,
he humbled himself
and became obedient to death—even
death on a cross!

Therefore . . .

do everything without complaining or arguing, so that you may become blameless and
pure, children of God without fault in a
crooked and depraved generation, in which
you shine like stars in the universe.

Philippians 2:7–8, 14–15

Father,
I am a servant.
I want to be a faithful servant,
not grumbling or complaining,
not arguing over your directions,
but trusting your wisdom
to know what you are doing
and eager to cooperate with my part
of the task.
May I look to you all the time,
alert to your smallest signal
that points me toward what you want me
to do.

20

"REASSURE ME"

For I am convinced that neither death nor life,
neither angels nor demons, neither the present
nor the future, nor any powers, neither height
nor depth, nor anything else in all creation,
will be able to separate us from the love of
God that is in Christ Jesus our Lord.

Romans 8:38–39

Libby stayed overnight at our house one
night. After lights were out, she whispered,
"I'm afraid someone will come and take me
away from my mommy." Terrifying news of
kidnappings filters through to these children.

Once when our grandson Cliff was with
us, he needed to go to the boys' restroom in
a shopping mall. As his grandfather walked
with him, Cliff said seriously, "You do know
about strangers, don't you?" He was only
four years old; his parents had already cau-
tioned him about dangers in public places.

Horrors happen. Children need constant reassurance that those whom they trust will protect them. But no horror can rob us of the love of God in Christ Jesus. Even as a hen gathers her chicks under her wings, and even as a grandmother draws her granddaughter close to her in the dark, so God surrounds us in the darkness and assures us of his love.

Of what use is this eternal love if there is no immediate protection or closeness for some children? Children are snatched from those they love. We cannot understand how God allows that, but we do know that in God's view, the snatching is only for the moment, as awful as that moment is. The love of God is forever.

Children in distress cry for their mothers and their fathers. Children of God in their distress cry for their Father, and he is there.

> We walk as children in a dark and strange room. We can't see our way around the corners or the obstacles, but we sense a presence. God's hand holds ours, and he has confided in us. He has told us his intimate, everyday name—Emmanuel—God with us.
>
> Gerhard Frost

> And surely I am with you always.
>
> Matthew 28:20

Father,
    In our frightening world,
we don't know how to reassure the children.
    We fear what we don't understand,
and there is a lot that we don't understand.
    In the words of another teacher, I pray:
        "Who am I to show the way
            day by day
            to little children?
        I so prone to go astray . . .
    Let the children see the teacher,
leaning strong on Thee" (Source unknown).

21

BLESS THEM

I praise you because I am fearfully and
wonderfully made;
your works are wonderful.
Your eyes saw my unformed body.

Psalm 139:14, 16

God saw all that he had made, and it was
very good.

Genesis 1:31

Young Josh, twelve years old, crippled by
cerebral palsy and developmentally disabled,
was battered by a demented stepmother and
left to die alone under an abandoned house.
His teachers and friends at school loved
him. They admired his valiant struggles to
manage his life. No one knew of the abusive
treatment he received at home until his body
was discovered. It was small comfort, but his
friends knew that in school, at least, he had
been blessed, not battered.

A five-year-old child, classified as emotionally handicapped, dawdled behind the other members of his group as they walked down the school hallway. His teacher repeatedly urged him, "Keep up!" Finally he looked up at her and chanted in a sing-song voice, "You'll get me fast, you'll get me slow, but you'll never get me normal!"

Laughing, his teacher thought, *Normal? Maybe not, but I can certainly accept him as unique!*

Do my students feel battered—or blessed?

Rejected—or accepted?

Peculiar—or unique?

When a developmentally disabled child is born, according to Stanley Hauerwas, professor of ethics at Duke University, the question we should ask is not "Why does God permit mental retardation in his world?" but "What sort of community should we become so that mental retardation need not be a barrier to a child's enjoyment of a gratifying life?"

In our schools we worry about physical comfort: heat, lights, seats, sound systems— and we must be concerned about each of those things. As Jesus said about external meticulousness: "These you ought to have done, but *not by leaving the more important things undone*" (Matt. 23:23 author's paraphrase).

How often is a child made to feel very uncomfortable, not because of physical factors, but because of individual differences or "deficiencies" as perceived by the teacher or peers?

Can we only bless those children who are whole? Can we give positive strokes only to those who please us? Can we not see that emotionally battered child and bless him or her also? The law says we must accept them, these children with exceptionalities. But the labels, once applied, are difficult to overlook.

When I began teaching, I did not have recent training in intelligence testing. I did not realize the pervasive stigma attached to "the unsuccessful learner." I was surprised to hear teachers thank me for taking these "impossible students" out of their classes and tell me, "You'll never be able to do anything with them."

At the end of that first semester, one of the students wrote to me, "I now believe that I am more than I thought I was when I came into this class." She was a beautiful young woman whose face was drawn into lines of deep-seated unhappiness. I saw her countenance lighten up as she began to be successful in learning.

God has not labeled me "failure," even though I have failed. He has not labeled me "slow learner," even though I am grievously slow in learning what he teaches me. He is patient with me, with my repeated failures, with my slow learning of basic truths about himself, and most of all, he never gives up on me. Can I do less in my classroom?

Gary Smalley in *The Gift of the Blessing* details five elements of blessing: meaningful touch, the spoken word, the expression of high value, the description of a special future, and the application of a genuine commitment to assist in bringing about that special future. For our own children and our students, these factors are essential in making sure that they receive our gift of the blessing.

Blessed is he who has regard for the weak.
Psalm 41:1

Father,
Thank you that you never give up on me—
weak, failing, slow to learn.
You, the perfect teacher,
must take a lot of time to repeat the lesson.
Let me not do less
for these whom you have given me
to teach.

22

DISCIPLINE ME

My son, do not regard lightly
   the discipline of the Lord,
nor lose courage when you
   are punished by him.
For the Lord disciplines him whom he loves,
and chastises every son whom he
   receives. . . .
For the moment all discipline seems painful
rather than pleasant; later it yields the peace-
ful fruit of righteousness to those who have
been trained by it.

Hebrews 12:5, 11 RSV

Kristen is in the first grade. She loves her teacher very much; she sometimes even spends the night with her teacher when her mother has to be out of town.

88

Recently the teacher had to raise her voice to another student who was not behaving well. Kristen immediately went to the other child, put her arm around her, and said gently, "She isn't being mean to you; she just wants you to learn."

God's voice sounds harsh sometimes too, when he must shout to get our attention. But he isn't being mean to us; he just wants us to learn!

Good discipline is integral to the teaching process, in the classroom and in life. Discipline does not equal punishment; discipline involves suffering the consequences of bad decisions, but it is actually training, or "breaking in." A skilled trainer can take a wild horse and bring him under control. Discipline includes learning to trust the wisdom and the motives of the trainer.

Jesus gathered twelve men around him as his disciples—those whom he would discipline. He questioned them often, reassured them frequently, demonstrated what he wanted them to do, and encouraged them to look beyond his departure to the time when they would be in charge of the work he left behind. The disciples Jesus left behind did not appear to be promising candidates for leadership, but Jesus had trained them well. He

then sent to them the Holy Spirit to be their
constant counselor and guide. The disciples
were disciplined to obey the Lord they loved
with their whole hearts. They had learned the
wisdom of obedience.

The fear of the LORD is the beginning of
knowledge,
but fools despise wisdom and discipline.
Proverbs 1:7

Father,
I want to be your obedient disciple.
That will mean submitting to
your discipline,
your training.
Forgive me that too many times
you have had to shout to get my attention.
Tune me in to the still small voice
you use to guide me in the right paths
when I get quiet enough to listen.
Your discipline is born of love
and deep understanding.
You know when I go astray;
You understand why I go astray.
Thank you for the depths
of your knowledge and understanding;

*thank you for your unlimited patience
and faithfulness.
Grant to me an understanding heart
and discerning wisdom
when I face the problems of my students
so that I, too, can speak kindly and firmly,
with authority and truth,
undergirded with love.*

23

ACCEPT THE GIFT

God can do anything, you know—far more than you could ever imagine or guess or request in your wildest dreams! He does it not by pushing us around but by working within us, his Spirit deeply and gently within us.

Ephesians 3:20 *The Message*

Students often bring presents for the teacher. Some of my favorites have been personal, like the needlepoint picture of two goldfinches perched on a thistle made for me by a former seventh-grade student. She delivered the gift years after I taught her, still remembering that I liked goldfinches.

Other gifts are practical, such as tools for a carpenter or kitchen utensils for a cook. Some gifts are paradoxical. Once we were given a piece of heavy brass and I said, "It's beautiful! What is it?" I have enjoyed using the doorstop ever since, but I had no idea what it was. We dream of extravagant gifts and sometimes even receive them.

The perfect gift says something about the personality of the giver and also matches the wishes and needs of the receiver. That kind of gift leads to cries of pleasure: "It's just like Nan to give me that! It's exactly what I needed!"

God's gift of Jesus expressed his own nature and is *exactly* what we needed.

When I look at my students, what would I like to give them? What exactly do they need?

Suppose we could provide a safe magic potion that would go steadily to work and begin to change students from the inside out, correcting difficult behaviors, clearing up learning problems, healing emotional wounds, strengthening self-concepts, building positive attitudes, giving patience and self-discipline, satisfying the need to belong and the need for meaning. How difficult would it be to market such a remedy?

Jesus offers such a gift. When he told a woman in Samaria about his offer of water to completely and finally quench thirst, she begged him for it (John 4). She found what she had thirsted for—an acceptance and a life-changing force from the only one who could provide what she needed.

In Jack Finney's novel *Time and Again* the protagonist, Si Morley, speaks of his generation as "constantly seeking, with a hollow at the core that is never filled." This longing comes from the innate knowledge that God *is*, contradicted by a refusal to glorify God or give thanks to him (Rom. 1:21).

In the children's book *Old Turtle*, Douglas Wood imagines the newly created creatures of the world beginning to argue about God until Old Turtle says, "God is all that we dream of, and all that we seek, all that we come from and all that we can find. God IS." Later in the book, the people who came into the world also argued about God until "the people could not remember who they were, or where God was . . . and after a long, lonesome and scary time . . . the people listened, and began to hear . . . and Old Turtle smiled. . . . And so did God."

We are in a long, lonesome, and scary time when God is forgotten among many, yet "to all who received him, to those who believed in his name, he gave the right to become children of God" (John 1:12).

This gift of Jesus, once received, works slowly, beginning that "good work in us" that is God's plan in operation. We cannot push our world, or our students, into God's kingdom. But we can trust God to show them his great gift.

> For it is God who works in you to will and to act according to his good purpose.
>
> Philippians 2:13

> He who began a good work in you will carry it on to completion until the day of Christ Jesus.
>
> Philippians 1:6

Father,
I need this gift for myself.
I thank you that you have given Jesus
as the power to work in us
what is pleasing in your sight.
I pray for my students:
those who are troubled
in mind and in spirit,
those who flounder
in confusion and rebellion,

seeking that which will change them
into what they think they want to become.
May my life show them Jesus.
Work in them deeply and quietly
that work of your Spirit
who alone can draw them to yourself.

24

DON'T BE ABSURD!

He who has ears, let him hear.

Matthew 11:15

Therefore everyone who hears these words of mine and puts them into practice is like a wise man who built his house on the rock. But everyone who hears these words of mine and does not put them into practice is like a foolish man who built his house on sand.

Matthew 7:24, 26

As Henri Nouwen states in *Devotional Classics,* the word *absurd* comes from the Latin word *surdus,* which means "deaf." The word *obedient* has the same root as *audire* in Latin, which means "to listen." An absurd life, then, is a life that refuses to listen, an attitude that rejects obedience.

Nouwen goes on to say that to keep ourselves from absurdity, we have to find ways to prevent the world from filling our lives to such an extent that there is no place left to listen. In that way we can move from an absurd life with its noisy worries to an obedient life that is attentive and provides inner space in which to listen. We can become "all ears" for God.

An alarming number of students now are diagnosed with an attention deficit disorder. In an effort to improve student performance on academic tasks, medications such as Ritalin are prescribed to help children focus their attention. Teachers and parents often can tell exactly when the medication wears off because the students have difficulty listening and following instructions.

Jesus often told his followers, "Listen to me." He wanted to give them important instruction. His relationship with his followers was like that of sheep with a shepherd. In fact, he called himself "the good shepherd" to emphasize the type of relationship he had with those who followed him.

The people Jesus taught were familiar with the relationship between sheep and their shepherd. In Palestine, sheep were raised primarily for their wool; they remained with their shepherd for several years. They came to know and understand his voice and the distinctive language he used with them. He called sharply from time to time to remind them of his presence. When they heard his voice, they followed him, but if a stranger called, they would stop short and lift up their heads in alarm. If the call of the stranger was repeated, the sheep would turn and run away.

After the resurrection, as Mary stayed in the garden, distraught at the disappearance of Jesus' body, he came to her, but she did not recognize him until he called her name. When she heard "Mary" in that unforgettable voice, she knew that he was indeed Jesus. He was her shepherd.

Like sheep, we are very dependent on the voice of the shepherd to direct us and to keep us away from danger. Listen to the Shepherd's voice for direction, for instruction. And remember that to the students, you also are a shepherd.

> My sheep listen to my voice; I know them, and they follow me.
>
> John 10:27

Father,
    My life has often been absurd,
        unheeding, tuned out, deaf.
        Like an unruly sheep,
        I have gone my own way.
Thank you that you always call me back.
    You have trained my ears to listen
        and my heart to respond.
Forgive me that I am easily distracted
        and fail to hear your voice.
Heal my "attention deficit disorder"
        so that I can pay attention
            to what you say to me.

25

"CHERISH ME"

But blessed is the man who trusts in the
     LORD,
  whose confidence is in him.
He will be like a tree planted by the water
  that sends out its roots by the stream.
It does not fear when heat comes;
  its leaves are always green.
It has no worries in a year of drought
  and never fails to bear fruit.
                    Jeremiah 17:7–8

On an extended trip west we drove into
the San Juan Mountains of Colorado and
spent the night near Box Canyon in Ouray.
Water poured down the side of the canyon
into a rocky stream outside our window.

Morning brought bright sunshine. We
walked up a gravel road toward the canyon

and looked down at the tumbling water in the stream. There beside the turbulence, protected by a huge, jagged rock, was a perfectly formed evergreen tree. Its branches feathered out into lacy fans that brushed the earth around its roots, which tapped deeply into the constantly flowing stream of water.

We were told that each year an average of twenty-six inches of snow and forty inches of rain fall there, saturating the ground, filling the stream, and watering the luxuriant foliage all around.

Later that day we drove out of the mountains and stopped at a rest area fifty miles away. Set apart by rough, protecting wire were five scraggly little trees planted in the hard-packed, dry, cracked earth on the edge of the small roadside picnic area.

A neat sign was posted by the little trees:

Spare a cup of water for a little tree like me.

We only had one quart of water in our cooler. I wanted to haul water from everywhere and splash it all over those dry patches of dirt. I wanted to pour water like Elijah did on Mt. Carmel, gallons of water, until the ground was full and the water poured all over the parking lot. I wanted to snatch those little trees up, take them to Box Canyon, and find places for them beside that perfect tree that had all the protection and nourishment it needed.

But I could not move the trees or give them enough water to soak their roots. I had to keep on going. I could only hope that every traveler at that roadside stand would "spare a cup of water" for each of those little spruce trees.

When I travel that way again, I hope I will see them watered and growing, flourishing where they were planted, in a tough and challenging place.

In the same way, I see children who are cherished and protected, nourished in every possible way, and they are beautiful beyond description. I see other children, in shelters for the homeless, struggling to survive on cups of water poured occasionally over the parched ground of their lives. These children also are indescribably beautiful, with the potential to overcome and flourish.

I want my classroom to become a flowing stream from which young roots can draw deeply of the water that sustains their growth. I want my classroom to be a place in which every child knows that he or she is beautiful.

How many Flowers fail in Wood—
Or perish from the Hill—
Without the privilege to know
That they are Beautiful—
Emily Dickinson

He has made everything beautiful in its time.
Ecclesiastes 3:11

Father-Creator,
You designed the earth and everything in it
and filled it with great beauty.
Thank you for perfect trees
and for scraggly trees
that send their roots deep into the ground
in search of water.
Thank you for the soaring mountains
and the sprawling deserts,
each with its own life and beauty.
Thank you for the children.
May each of them know
that all of them are beautiful
in your eyes.

26

PLAN FOR THE FUTURE

For God did not give us a spirit of timidity, but a spirit of power, of love and of self-discipline.
2 Timothy 1:7

A spirit of cowardly fear looks into the future and whispers, "What will happen if . . ."

A spirit of power looks into the future and shouts, "I am confident of this very thing— that God will triumph!"

When we bog down in today's tasks, we are tempted to look into the future and complain, "Of what use is what I am doing today?"

In a pre-Easter service, the minister held up a rough-hewn nail and said, "What happens to a man's work when it is finished? How might this nail be used?

To build the temple?

To build a stable to shelter animals and the Christ?

To build coffins—or crosses?
To nail a criminal to a cross?"

The man who made the rough nails that were used when Jesus died had no inkling of the outcome of his work. If he had known, would it have made a difference?

All of us need to take pride in our work, but none of us can control the ultimate outcome or use of what we do or make.

What will our students do with what we teach them? How will they use the knowledge they have gained?

When a program for gifted students began in his school, David quickly excelled in math. His sixth-grade teacher said, "I have taught him all the math I know. He must have a teacher who can take him further." She saw that his need was met.

David began to move rapidly through the math courses available in the local high school and continued advanced instruction at one university during the school year and at another university in the summer months. What would he do with all that math knowledge and the computer technology he also mastered?

After he finished college and entered graduate school, he returned to participate in a teacher workshop at his local high school. "I will be teaching math courses during my graduate work; I want to learn how to teach," he said.

I must see my students not only as they are but also as what they can become. Some will become teachers too. If it is true that "we teach as we have been taught," they will to some extent model their teaching after ours. Should they follow the example I have set in the classroom? More importantly, though, should my students, regardless of their professions, live as they have seen me live?

Paul said, "Follow my example, as I follow the example of Christ" (1 Cor. 11:1). Can we dare to say that?

As teachers we want to teach

> with authority
>> with humility
>>> with openness
>>>> with insight
>>>>> with excitement
> powerfully
>> patiently
>>> persistently
> in a challenging way
>> in a way that disciplines
>>> in a way that provides what
>>> students need
> And above all these, we want to
> teach with love.

As teachers, at times our tasks and responsibilities are far greater than our own powers. But as teachers in Christ, we can believe that he will use whatever we offer in ways we may not even recognize.

> Take my yoke upon you, and learn from me, for I am gentle and humble in heart, and you will find rest for your souls.
>
> Matthew 11:29

> I have set you an example that you should do as I have done for you.
>
> John 13:15

Master teacher,
> *Grant that I may become*
> *the kind of teacher*
> *who will reflect*
> *your love*
> *in every place.*

Marjory Goldfinch Ward, formerly an assistant professor at Columbia College and an adjunct professor of gifted education at the University of South Carolina, has over twenty years' experience in public education. She is the author of *Who Will Be My Teacher?*